The Renfrew Road

Jim Ferguson

Urban Free Press

Glasgow 2018

www.jimfergusonpoet.co.uk

Contents

Cover art: Louise Malone
Design and typesetting by Fred Engels

ISBN: 978-1-9995921-1-0

Also by Jim Ferguson:

The Pine-Box-Jig Involves no Dancing: Extracts from the Diary of a Scottish Hippy

Punk Fiddle: a novel

The art of catching a bus and other poems

For Eva (poems: Famous Seamus Publishing)

When Feeling Fully at Home in the Drifting Living Room of Time (poems: Famous Seamus Publishing)

The Renfrew Road

yes   it may
or may it not

be after four

and there may be
no sunrise

anymore

five lives in one

there's my real life
and my dream life

and other lives
all intertwined

but i don't like
yet i do like

when it all
gets mixed up

inside

i am a profound
merchant banker

i am woman
i am man

i'm beyond all plans
of humans, of gods

and of alien dreams
i don't quite understand

i love the pink pound
i love excess unbound

get wide with me
i'll pummel and shaft

you're little working-class arse
til pained and broken you'll scream

oh little bunny... scream!
—

there's my old friend Dan
he's a very dead man
he's a clansman wha died at glencoe
he a native ameri-can
can do kin kinda man
he's a ghost wha can travel in time

—

there's my new friend Diane
she's a girls' kinda man
she can go in the clubs
all night long, she can dance
she can sing, do astronomy too
can right run riot right thru Theresa's Cunt

And Theresa's Cunt is the best night club

any body   ever   ever   knew

has landing strip   has helicopter pad

has a needle that points to the north
just in case some poor migrant gets lost

—

travelling light
just passport

and toothbrush
we don’t stop

for respite

the toothbrush
can open

all
borders,
fences,
people
and doors

while the passport
keeps everything

all
bright,
white
and clean
live your dream, live your dream, live your d r e a m-mmmmmm

—

Danny long-hair
ghosts along the road

a diabetic man
with a vision

and a plan
for the future

—

a street guru
on a brand new day

with battered guitar
and something to say

about dreaming revolution
and a Scotland that's free

of the dirty old hands
of the aristocracy

and the british royal family on the bbc
thrice nightly

at least
we all know our places

let's dream our way free
from the ugly faces

of our narcissistic rulers
and their white-washed history

of egotists and chauvinists
and a grovelling, self-serving

swarm of academics
who sell us british dreams

as the history of our rulers
who were all in fact enchanting and charming

and could never break a law
because all the rules of law they had approved

—

and the Renfrew Road is long
and common life is shorter

than expectation
would suggest

work and want and corporate
man-u-fact-urers

steal seconds of our breath
every second from our caves

and their fashion sense
much outshines our own

—

Miss Diane
she has frocks

that will blast off your socks
and she'll suck those bent cocks

any old time—
she snort high grade cocaine

out the window
from a thimble in the rain

she can massage the stars
she can take you to Mars

and all other destinations un-named
cause it's one law for her

while the rest sit oppressed
naked beneath blankets in prisons

with their little tiny coughs
with the cuffs on or off

little choice but what the guards give and take—

Diane she can dance
she can rant rave and trance

morning papers to wrap the poor dead paupers
serve them up on the pier

serve them straight, monk or queer
serves them right for being very very poor

serves them all right,
all those worthless little whores

the doors to their dreams are all closed
now

Harry Haller he don't dance here no more
he barred from Theresa's Cunt

for a fashion offence
and being a curious man—
poor Harry, poor Harry, poor Hermann

trees

there's pop
and there's rock

there's the private sector too
it's the glue holding all strands together

there's wood to burn
and there is access to guns

and rockets that can pin-point the dead

we can scurry and climb
sit aloft all sublime

with our feet on the decks
of our loving old oligarchs' yachts

we have branches
we have networks
we have a mentality
that rains down like leaves in your mind

we know your devices
we know where you've been
what you like, what you hate
what you've seen

no one's spying on you
that's a paranoid view

and you have only one body
to live your life through

we know who you are, we know what you do
we know exactly when you're going to die

—

Canadian something
tree with a massive trunk
see it on your tube
you know you've been there
with no one watching

red wood
dead wood
hard wood cock
word association
all comes back
sexual needs
we can exploit

prise from
your grubby dumb hands
every little penny
that you ever held dear
give us it

give us it in plain sight
thers's nothing of the night about us
for us your time does not exist
because your money
because your love
because your state of mind
has ceased to be your own
all of it, all of it, is ours alone

—

think yure an Inuit
think yure an ice-hugger
think yure melting underneath an over-ripe sun
there's a layer of plastic scum floating on the sea
and there's nowhere for carbon
there just aren't enough trees

think yure corned beef
think yure palm oil
think yure unrelenting desire for ancient timber
shiver shiver cold outside as you're fleeing from the sur
in the north you're most unwelcome
they want you all right back from where you've come

you can live in a tree-house
live a free life free from doubt
little insects crawling round you
not a problem in the north
you can squirt them dead
with chemical sprays and guns
what fun!

—

huge green arms
wave at the puny humans

waiting for the two-legged monsters
to stride forward in their damned-apocalypse style

they think it is something
to chip away a little bark

with letters from their
higher level of reason

their alpha-betti-spaghetti
or their chain-saw massacres

that help no one at all
perhaps it's only they who glide to suicide

childish drugs

off our heads
with reproduction
and the new asexual
brand of twenty-four-hour
machine-sex

like those old games
we used to play
President Evil
and
Hunt the Cunt
shooting them down
getting reward points
to spend at *Shemazing Online Everything*
brand or no brand
lawless liberty

it's that thing
we used to do in Spring
sneak under the rafters
beams of sunlight
reveal spider traces
as we move
through an attic dreamworld
of newborn maps and stories
dreams translucent all-sex   never money
money was just for the old
and we had none anyway
- we had none anyway

20 billion
almost human
stalking the planet
mass extinction everywhere
and still we fuck and fight
murder street illegals day and night
but we are infectious
breeders
smothering tight
every natural surface
it's possible for us to cover

we are the everything of planet-e

history lessons

when William Wallace fell off his horse
the monks of Paisley Abbey of course
did not rush to help a lowly horse thief

no matter that he was a good thief
on the right side of jesus
on the right side like a Scottish Robin Hood

the birds sang in the trees
their words the weight of light
while humanity stuffed its ears to dull the tune

under the gaze of god the father
under the guidance of jesus the son
deluded monotheists all for one

Diane she lifted her fingers
and Dan he twinkled his toes
as from rough pasture Wallace the bold arose

chanting: freedom, freedom, freedom
for all, for liberty i'll answer the call
drink whisky until the day of doom

hark now boys the thistle's in bloom
arise from your hunger arise
and delirious enter the tomb

with conscience clear
and clouds overhead
quartered in your gory bed

with warm heart beating red
tossed aloft to feed the dogs
what are we doing here?

nothing but food for the trees
vessels for shipping disease
a plague upon the house of mother earth

when someone snorted and laughed
piled the bodies up on the cart
and the donkey entered Jerusalem

proclaiming love and peace at last
peace and love at last
peace, dead peace, at last

peace at last

that's entertainment

by way of greek and roman amphitheatre
any space became an arena for laughter or war

humans holding no notion of what they are for
hacked at flesh with lethal swords

dreaming the blood was recompense
for the cruelty of their deeds and words

that no alternative, nothing new, sun
shone in the sky with a mocking light

but couldn't put anything right

drowned in a broth of metaphors
still no-one knew what they were for

dance to remember and dance to forget
tied to each body a single mind

ever pulled to pleasure sublime
escaping the roots of the earth

that were much too cruel to live with
—much too cruel to live with

the reverie in the stars our only comfort
celebrities wank on their own words

what good fortune!

laugh to remember and laugh to forget
the past and the future and every regret

out of our minds with mechanical sex
yearning to lose our *self* in joys unbound—

and filled with awe inspiring
ridiculousness William Wallace stood up

got back on his horse
and rode away

breeders

the road crumble and decayed
fewer people walked its way
corpses piled on off-ramps
wounded stragglers in transit camps

others elsewhere formed a mini-state—
called it Cotland and they tried to generate
children

a nation of infants
who
knew not what to do
as many women died in childbirth
stupid men following their cocks
foraged for food

while others, enraged,
destroyed and desecrated
all works of art
offensive to their eyes

—

it was May
when the cygnets appeared

in alliance with the trees
they were talking revolution

to overthrow the old regime
of the squalid infectious humans

the older swans were unconvinced
of necessity for action

for left to themselves alone
humans were all bound for putrefaction

not so, said the cygnets
and the trees sadly agreed

as they had misplaced affections
for those damned and upright monkeys

they had loved the silly sounds
of human songs

and enjoyed their rotting corpses
bringing fly and migde and raptor

curtail relentless desert's
northward march

—

and the Renfrew Road
is a long road

but no one knows or cares
where it is

where it's going
or where it's been

soon everything
will be unseen by any living human eyes

no more who, no more where
and no more why

and the trees don’t want to meet
their cacti cousins

no more accidental deaths
ghostbirds flying into glass

or minced up in them windmill’s
bloody arms

no more plastic   no more reason
no more   naming of the seasons

no more time
no more mythic gods and sods

and no more proclamations
that rise above the wind

with ape-mammalian power
never again, ever, cometh the derangement of the hour

or of glass, synthetic compounds
or devil-dogs bred merely for their looks

no more purple   no more ermine
no more condescending sermons

spurting wryly from religion’s purple cock-head
warmly welcome the human and the dead

human and dead
all the one and same

all unreal and rational
all that is rational is unreal

that's the deal the floating
universe beyond our comprehension

made with itself

only fucking in the name of its very own survival
nothing that those paltry human minds could ever rival

even with elaborate dancing
and ever more pointless appeals

to collective innocence
contained within an unseen collective strength

of the very same universal essence, hence
cometh the war, cometh the hour

cometh the cygnet, cometh the tree
cometh the crazy-dancing-human-monkey-tree

we aren't all capitalists now
we aren't all Americans now
we aren't any thing at all now
once breeders, now bringers

of their own special darkness
that they called their own extinction
wave good-bye humanity
let's all wave humanity good-bye

what if the conscious mind tends to nihilism – and so our bodies evolved to find sex pleasurable, to ensure we kept up our end and gave our end away? the figure of the celibate monk... rarely drunk.

forgetting atoms dance

how could we be
so naive, Kathy Acker said,
forgetting she was dead
already
Diane and Dan
were dressed to go
in to-to action in stereo
with Kathy a glowing orb
between cunt and cock
and much too dead to shock

Dan had donned
his Native American shaman attire
acquired back in '97
knowing it was the only
counter-cultural empire
worth emulation
his inspiration hailed
from the north
how had they survived
the European invasion
that rubbed about everything out

Diane wore a boiler
suit industrial
sexless faxshion
they scrambled
to The Mall—
it was shut
ring-fenced
due to the war
it was usless
to even try to enter
the edifice
didn’t know what it was for
—a worldly wonderful pyramid
stuffed with rotten
consumer non-durables
protected by soldiers and guards

instead
they head
along to the morgue
which nestles
on the bank
of a dried river-bed
here there’s
a queue
of desperate
sad faces
seeking
the corpes
of friends
acquaintances
lovers
family members
disappeared queers
grannies

automatons
things and people like that

others are
curious
tourists
out to gloat
at the fate
that had not yet
thrust itself
upon them

Diane whispered into Dan's deaf ear
I'm hoping you will fuck me here
Dan did not reply or notice
just how nicely Diane smiled

she'd whispered into his dead-nerved ear
how could he be expected to hear
though he felt her breath
caress his auld jawbone

his cock stirred in his pants
and he thought he might
like to fuck Diane right here
right now

every woman was an object
in post-capitalist corporate
Renfrew Road
every man refused to understand

that if all women were objects
then all men were objects too

a spectrum of genders
but sex required no spectrum
merely objects, required objects
power
and
exploitation
and
murder
an infinite
appetite
for objects
all kinds
of objects
to use as fuck-toys
armies of landlords
fuck out the brains
of vulnerable
human monkeys
dancing round
their discount cards
singing
we are all objects too
we are all objects too

—

alcoholic necrosis
murdering souls
amphetamine
bleeding gums
guns at the ready
here come the scum-jake-pensioner-kids

and scientists
study the juices
emitted by bacterial infection
of the limbs
and send them in
to outer-space
to fend for themselves
as offensive space weapons
waging war against
the universe itself

—

in a cellular world
of innerspace

introspection
is the only road to follow

—

are we that part of nature
only striving to destroy

with our misanthropic melancholy songs

self obsessive suicidal cock-cunts
how could we be

how could we be
*how could **we** be*

so naive
Kathy Acker said, so beautifully
she understands
'blood and guts in high-school'
isn't really fiction
under guns

there's nothing new,
it seems,
over the sun

at
the
end
of
the
rain
bow — no one gonny rush in and save us

anywhere else
there is this
that
and
the
other

who is the other?

sitting still

now, this body — this body, now

that i occupy — with more ease and comfort

than once was the way — runs on its own strength

to get through the day — but says much less than it used to want to sa

by way of complaint, protest and such
and that awful sickness made me run
for the white of the bathroom and the upsurge of puke
that no kind of book was ever going to fix

no weird learning to unlock the mind
just let the body do its thing
and spend time hoping
'the future will be different'

while courage comes to gaze,
look through the window with its nose to the glass
and when it leaves there's a mark on the pane,
let ideas grow, courage come around again

and this will be the day
my body gets comfortable in itself and with time—
its passing and its iceberg nature—
the past all under water and the future

piercing — bright, reaching for one vast, open sky
grey sky, blue sky, pink sky, orange sky, yellow sky
a sky to stretch — my eager body over — and across the rainbow
to get there and take it — make it mine, my body

now — this body — this body now — alive

—

sunsets so spectacular
forgetting atoms
dance
the nothing new

—

ansaphone poems

hello
is that you urizit that machine thing
ach fuck that
beep
phone me back

**

hello there
jist been up tae see ma grandpa
eez dayn that stan laurel thing again
ye kin alwiz tell
eez hudda few haufs
whinih diz that
anywey
hi wiz chattin away
fuhlla life
the auld fucker
amazin really
anywey
cheerio the noo.

**

we are calling
to inform you
about a new
government
heating initiative

**

gutta knock back
ye in
ye hear me
gutta knock back
n thull no serve mi
gonny you go doon
get uz a boattla whisky
n sum fags
they widny even geemi the fags
um awright tae
fucking bastards
gonny you go doon
ach is that that fuckin machine am tokin tae
canny believe they widny sell mi fags
i'm 62
think they know whut age ah um
how auld dae ye need tae be
tae buy fags anyway
a knock back eh
no hud wanna them fur years
no furra.

**

we are calling
to inform you
about a new
government
awareness initiative

we wish to let you know
that we are aware
that you are unaware

please be aware
that it is in all of our interests
to be aware

**

ahv loast ma keys
thir somewhere in the hoose
fuck knows where
I must've hud thum ir ah widny uv goat in here

kin you nip doon n gehtus wan cut
how much dae ye think it might cost
a fiver? merr than a fiver?
ahl geeyi money furra bevy anaw

**

hello mister ferguson
this is Carla speaking from the Royal Bank
on Alexandra Parade
Just to let you know
that the claim that you put in has been successful
and the cash has been credited to your account

it is now available to you,
thank you very much,
bye.

**

hello

winter comes
a fearsome killer

through the aged
darkening day

youth is busy
with its snowballs

struggling old folk
hidden away

**

howyi doin there
ah heard ye wur back the other night
geeza phone whin ye get this...

oh right ahv goat a new mobile number
I canny remember whit it is
so ahl huvtae phone ye back later

awright, ahv goat a day aff the morra
hope tae seeyi furra pint
if yir up furrit

**

hello mister ferguson
this is Carla speaking from the Royal Bank
on Alexandra Parade

Just to let you know
that the claim that you put in has been unsuccessful
and the funds recently deposited by us
into your account
have now been deducted from your account

we are sorry
for any inconvenience
bye.

**

do you need
replacement
windows and doors

do you need
prosthetic teeth or limbs
funeral insurance
electric wheelchair
enter our raffle
and receive a free
gift write right
ink pen
with synchronised nib

let me stress
we are not Microsoft, Google or Facebook
this is a genuine offer
please enter your offer code
at www dot scammers-un-limited dot com

**

hello --- aye
jist tae let yi know
Rab died
that's him
gone
eh --- aye
ah hudny heard frae um
fur aboot two year either
last message hi sent mi
hi wiz askin 'is Fergie still a wanker?'
that's you innit
well uryi
uryi still a wanker?
ah don't know
layter man --- layter
ahl be in touch wae the funeral details
cheerio

**

you propose to kill yourself once
but, bitch
i kill myself everyday
I am a Turner canvas,
a broken battleship, taken out
the knackers at the gunsho
flash of sunset —
I spit on it, from the
cleft of my variegat
palette, I am a deform
sort of mad hat
sitting on a
procession of se
portraits, and swilling the
colours. — and you
of suicide — yo
two bit bi
what do you know of Cassius —
you're a slip of Clay, you a go
in the shape of a cabbage p
kid — if you want to do it,
fickle bitch —
but don't talk of it
don't think that I'll think you
for it —
I'll play your eulogy
a kazoo —
I'll piss on the peonies f
blossom from your eye sockets